THE OTHER SIDE

Poems about medicine and the maladies that plague it

SWAPNIL PARALIKAR

Physiologist, educationist & poet

MD (Physiology),
FAIMER (CMCL-2015), ACME
Associate Professor,
Department of Physiology,
Government of Gujarat (Consortium),
GUJARAT, INDIA.

notionpress.com

INDIA • SINGAPORE • MALAYSIA

ISBN
Paperback 979-8-89588-268-9
Hardcase 979-8-89588-630-4

Devoted to

My mother, Mrs. Alka Paralikar,

*For recognizing my innate abilities and always being
with me through thick and thin*

My remote mentor, Dr. Upreet Dhaliwal

(former Director-Professor
of Ophthalmology at UCMS, Delhi)

For inspiring and guiding me to write better poetry

&

To my readers

(mainly medical educationists)

For appreciating my poems in conferences and workshops

Contents

Acknowledgement   *ix*

Foreword   *xi*

My Journey as a Poet   *xiii*

Preface   *xv*

I. MEDICINE

1. If A Doctor……   2

2. If a teacher...   4

3. The Physical-An Era Bygone   5

4. Murder of the Medical Educationist   7

5. Confusion Based Medical Education (CBME)   10

6. Doctors, Poetry and Empathy   12

7. The Stethoscope   14

8. Hospital   15

9. Cinquain- Caring, Chaos, Conflict   17

10. My first patient   21

11. Dear Student in Distress   24

12. My Protege   27

13. A Push to Freedom   31

14. Student X   33

15. Suicide   34

16. Beating Procrastination   35

II. MIND

17. Can I carry on? — 39
18. To Obsessive Compulsive Disorder — 41
19. During my blues — 44
20. Misery and Remedy — 47
21. To My Asperger's — 49
22. To Post-Traumatic Stress Disorder — 51
23. Amiss – A Cinquain — 53
24. The Fallout of Ruffled Feathers — 55
25. STIGMA — 57
26. Bye-Bye OCD-I (Cinquain) — 59
27. Bye-Bye OCD-II (Haiku) — 61

III. PANDEMIC

28. Awakening-I (Cinquain) — 63
29. Awakening-II — 65
30. Two men who met a different fate — 67
31. Loneliness — 70
32. My Corona diary — 72
33. White Curtain — 74

IV. METAPHORS

34. Ode to the Heart — 77
35. A Runner's Heart — 81
36. Ode to the Brain — 84

37. Cursed Commodity   85

38. The Il- Fated Patient   86

39. Ulcers   87

40. Physiology   89

41. The Organ Supreme   90

42. Genes: Miscreants meet their Match   92

43. Why do the Humanities Matter?   94

44. A Late Betrayal   96

45. Misery Unleashed by the Messenger   100

46. The College   103

47. The Resident   104

48. The Canteen   105

49. Teachers   106

50. The Exams   107

51. Baroreceptors   108

52. Fix the lecture   110

53. Rules for Power Point   113

54. Ode to CMCL FAIMER   115

55. Ode to Baroda   117

56. Health   119

Acknowledgement

I am grateful to

Dr. Rajesh Kathrotia and Dr. Chinmay Shah

Additional Professor, Department of Physiology, AIIMS, Rajkot

*Professor and Head, Department of Physiology,
Government Medical College, Bhavnagar (respectively)*

for their perennial support

I also thank my mentors`

Dr. BM Palan, Dr. Sunil Gupte
*(formerly Professor and Head of Psychiatry and former Dean at
NDMVPS, Nashik and my maternal uncle)* **&**

Dr. Hemant Mehta *(formerly Dean at GMC, Bhavnagar)*

for guiding and hand holding during turbulent years

I would also like to thank Dr. Balaji Ghughare, Dr. Rakesh Luhana, Dr. Anuradha Joshi, Dr. Purnima Barua, Dr. Juhi Kalra, Dr. Satendra Singh, Dr. Sanjoy Das, Dr. Vanita Lal Das, Dr. Bharti Mehta , Dr. Kavita Bhatnagar, Dr. Amir Khan Mahroof, Dr. Sumanth, Dr. Sukhinder Baidwan, Dr. Shuchi, Dr. Abhijeet Dutta, Dr. Gagan Bajaj, Dr. Hironmoy Roy, Dr. Narendra Pathak, Dr. Sumit Kapadia, and a host of others, for being with me through thick and thin, and appreciating my poetry.

This would be incomplete without thanking my father, Dr. Jagdish Paralikar, for his critical insights, my post-graduate teacher, Dr. MB Jani, and Dr. Sanjay Bedi (MEU India) for their love and support.

Foreword

Dr. Swapnil Paralikar is a teacher, a healer, a family man, a friend, a peer, and a poet. Years of practice at these roles have taught him not only compassion but have also given him deeper insight into the human condition, and into socio-cultural structures that impact the human condition.

This book is an ode to the gamut of experiences that have shaped the life of Dr. Swapnil Paralikar. In it you will find evidence of the full spectrum of human emotions - joy, struggle, optimism, suffering, pride and resilience. Be prepared to journey into the classroom, through corridors of hospitals, and into the minds of those who learn medicine, and those who practice it.

Medical science is no cakewalk. The learning and the practice environment are fast-paced and high-pressure, with little time for reflection. That is the reason that the experiences of people who provide healthcare deserves to be recorded, just as the experiences of the people who receive it – our patients – should be, and often are, chronicled. There is no richer source of profound emotional truth than a doctor's [or a patient's] story. The poems in this volume explore and articulate these truths in an honest and reflective way.

Dr Swapnil tells his story in verse – this is a powerful medium and it is a brave choice. Poetry offers a unique lens through which to explore life. Through poetry, we can give a voice to our feelings and emotions, to our unspoken fears, hopes, and vulnerabilities. Once vocalized, using imagery and metaphor, we can then examine our experiences and hope to find meaning, clarity, and comfort.

The medical profession demands a certain level of clinical detachment. This book, conversely, reminds us of the importance of connectedness, of communication, and of humanity. I encourage readers to approach the poems with an open mind and heart. They are sure to find comfort, inspiration, and meaning within these pages.

It has been an honor to witness Dr. Swapnil make his way as a poet, and I am privileged that he invited me to write the foreword to his book. I wish him all the best in his journey through life.

Dr. Upreet Dhaliwal, MS

Former Director-Professor of Ophthalmology,

University College of Medical Sciences,

University of Delhi

CMCL-FAIMER Fellow 2015
Foundation in Narrative-Based Medicine-2023,
Temerty Faculty of Medicine, University of Toronto
Editor - RHiME
Author of InVerse Medicine
Website: https://www.reetsingh.in

My Journey as a Poet

Poetry is a diary kept by a sea creature who lives on land, and   wishes he could fly- Carl Sandburg *(American poet and Pulitzer   Prize winner)*

I began writing poetry by accident after completing my medical studies. I was a person who wished to travel to distant lands, and fly. However, circumstances compelled me to stay put around my place of birth. The environment then was not conducive to writing and teaching oneself poetry.

A decade later I wrote some poems on the Google Group of the MUHS Advanced Course which I was pursuing in 2013. My co-learners appreciated the poems. I knew that I could write good poetry!

Then during the CMCL FAIMER session of 2015, I met the Editor-in-Chief of RHIME, Dr. Upreet Dhaliwal (Research and Humanities in Medical Education – www. Rhime.in). RHIME is an on-line journal and Asia's sole authentic journal devoted to medical humanities. With the aim of publishing in RHIME, I wrote a poem which was published *(A Runner's Heart)*. However, my big moment arrived in 2018 when I published the popular poem *'Murder of the Medical Educationist'* which was a fitting commentary on the state of medical education in the country then. I was now a budding poet!

Dr. Upreet Dhaliwal madam always insisted that she will publish only esoteric poems in RHIME. She always gave valuable feedback when she rejected my poems. The long -distance training under her led me to write six more sterling poems for RHIME. I consider her to be my Hattie Steinberg (Thomas Friedman's teacher at Minneapolis; Friedman took only one journalism class under her, yet he is one of the best Non-Fiction writers in the world and a New York Times columnist).

Then I wrote much better verse, be it- 'The Physical -An Era Bygone" 'To Obsessive Compulsive Disorder' 'Ode to the Heart' 'Awakening' (during CORONA Times), 'During my Blues' and dabbled into writing Cinquains and Haikus. Such a training-by-fire has culminated in the publication of this poetry compilation.

I hope you, my readers, find the poems worthy of your read.

Swapnil Paralikar

Preface

Poetry in medicine is a nascent phenomenon. It deems to illuminate medicine's artistic side. However, the 'The Other Side' explores my travails and tribulations as I meander through the glistening and at times gloomy, corridors of medicine.

Normally, a doctor examines a patient with a curtain to protect the latter's privacy. 'The Other Side' explores aspects behind the curtains that often go unnoticed and unheard. Poems of ideal values of a doctor and a teacher are followed by the maladies which plague medicine and medical education. I have also penned poems on the magnificence of the vital organs.

My tryst with mental health is dealt with eloquently. It is an honest rendition of an arduous journey to seek cure as I was plagued with a mental illness.

Because many poems were written during the Corona epidemic, there is a bold prediction that Corona will be beaten. Indeed, it was!

Medical teachers may use these poems as a trigger to teach Humanities and inculcate altruism, behavior, compassion, diversity and empathy in students.

The book is a solemn endeavor by me to pen my deepest thoughts and emotions in verse. I hope you peep into 'The Other

Side' with curiosity and compassion, and finally emerge more erudite about medicine's deepest truths.

Lastly, I finish with Emily Dickinson's famous poem:

This is my letter to the world,
That never wrote to me, -

The simple news that Nature told,
With tender majesty.

Her message is committed
To hands I cannot see;

For love of her, sweet countrymen,
Judge tenderly of me!

Emily Dickinson

I sincerely hope that you enjoy reading these poems as much as I loved writing them.

Dr. Swapnil Paralikar

MBBS, MD, FAIMER (CMCL-2015), ACME

I
MEDICINE

1

If A Doctor......

If you consult a doctor,

and he listens to you with open ears,

and he allows you to share all your queries and fears,

and he asks the right questions,

and he examines you with precision,

and he explains the cause of your ills,

and he elucidates all the available pills,

and he treats you with honor,

then he is truly the right doctor.

If you consult a doctor,

and he keeps your good in mind,

and he is soft and kind,

and is sympathetic to you,

and respects you,

and demonstrates excellence,

then he is truly a doctor,

true to his noble profession.

If you consult a doctor,

and he seems to possess all the know-how,

and is adept at his touch,

and shows the right care and concern,

and is mostly correct as much,

and is honest as such,

then you know he is competent and has the right conduct,

he is truly a doc,

a doctor with the highest standards.

2

If a teacher...

If a teacher teaches with passion,
and is true to his profession.
If he uses the latest pedagogy
and clears concepts that are foggy.
If he engages in scientific inquiry,
and even publishes it truly.
If he holds you up,
when everything around is bust.
If he mentors you honestly,
such that you make it finally.
If he is upright,
when circumstances don't seem right;
If he abides by these traits,
if he is a man of faith
Then he is truly a teacher,
who will touch your future.

3

The Physical-An Era Bygone

Auenbrugger tapped his father's half empty wine cellars,

and, thus, discovered percussion;

Laennec devised the stealthy stethoscope,

enabling the accurate probing of murmurs and holes;

A new era was ushered in,

the physical became a ritual:

between the doctor and his patient.

Now geeks with flashy tests and scans at their disposal,

skip the physical,

thereby diluting the ritual

between the doctor and his patient.

The physical has ebbed in stature and in spirit

Skipping it often leads to a diagnosis that is amiss.

In COVID times, the PPE kit and the mask are a barrier too brutal,

for the physical tends to be more ephemeral.

The doctor, a Martian man,

Treating without his touch and his scope;

It hardly bodes well for the physical,

which may soon belong to an era bygone!

(Paralikar, S. (2020). The physical - an era bygone. *Research and Humanities in Medical Education*, 7, 171. Retrieved from https://www.rhime.in/ojs/index.php/rhime/article/view/386)

4

Murder of the Medical Educationist

We've been in this profession
for some time now -
we like to think we teach well
 and are fair assessors too.

But then comes the question:
Are we as good as we can be?
Or should we try and evolve from
the old way of doing things?

I have tried new methods
that go against the flow.
I fall to my knees,
my ideas are knocked to the floor.

Red tape is stifling,
undermining, demotivating-
I have now become cynical,
and am bruised to the core.

I am trained to be
a sage on the stage;
but students plead
for a guide by the side.
I concede yet cannot
forgo my inheritance –
since I have severe
terminal Lecturitis.

My students are good at
rote learning, MCQ* solving,
but some are unfamiliar
with the English language.

When they define, during vivas,
glaucoma as high glucose, and
hemophilia as high hemoglobin –
how can I dream of PBLing** them?

I shudder to think of the
events that would unfold,
if my students were left
to think on their own.

Bulleted lists and paragraphs
make the work so easy -

conversely students, needing attendance,
fear death by power pointing.

The old school love vivas –
where looks and language rule;
the construct is dismantled,
and irrelevant factors confound.

Change is elusive and it's
not in my hands alone;
thus, the past will persist
as will the status quo,
calling death to the medical educationist.

*MCQ – Multiple Choice Question
**PBL – Problem-based Learning

(Paralikar, S. (2018). The Murder of the Medical Educationist. *Research And Humanities in Medical Education*, 5, 14–15. Retrieved https://www.rhime.in/ojs/index.php/rhime/article/view/171)

5

Confusion Based Medical Education (CBME)

There was the golden promise,
of molding global doctors.
Outcomes were laid down,
Laws framed for the better.
There was pomp and advertisement,
so followed faculty development:
Training in every facet,
teaching learning and assessment.

There were meetings and banter,
MEU* faculty at the center;
Just then new faculty were ignored,
principles of change management shown the door.

Faculty immersed in navigating
the steep demands:
Those who faltered, faced the reprimand.

Two years ago,
SDL**and ECE*** were the flavor,

only to see them recede,

into the back burner.

Then was the drama,

the curriculum became a pajama:

resolutions flowed thick and fast,

changes that just didn't last.

Now the system is in disarray,

students and faculty gone stray,

resolutions hold sway,

Confusion based medical education all the way!!

Medical Education Unit* Self Directed Learning* * Early Clinical Exposure***

6

Doctors, Poetry and Empathy

I

Students in hoards,

appear for the boards:

To become doctors,

that tend to the ill.

Yet they are still

amiss

in connecting with the ill.

This connection called empathy,

is for them a step too mighty!

II

Now robots,

will care for the sick.

Yet they cannot connect with ill.

The doctor can do so,

swith empathy,

his innate skill.

III

Those words that rhyme,

the poetry divine:

arouses emotions,

for the other humans.

Making one peep,

into his being.

They help to fill,

the void,

that robots provide:

Fostering this innate feeling,

that is empathizing!

(Joshi A, Paralikar S, Kataria S, Kalra J, Harkunni S, Singh T. Poetry in medicine: A pedagogical tool to foster empathy among medical students and health care professionals. Journal of Poetry Therapy. 2022 Apr 3;35(2):85-97.)

7

The Stethoscope

A breathless man's feeble voice,

demands the physician's attention;

It is the eerily stealthy stethoscope,

which detects his malady with precision.

Taking a cue, from boys playing with bamboo,

Laennec put it into wanton use.

Then it became the doctor's armor,

and the physician's reliable refuge.

There was an era not long gone,

when dubious docs dealt with the ill;

Came the stethoscope and thrived,

putting the nail in their cunning cabins.

It hears the heartbeats thud,

and the airways agonizingly ruffle,

the devout doctor now offers:

Hope and health to his precarious patients.

8

Hospital

A young man with fever, cough and weight loss,

meanders through the crowds

with his family in tow

worrying about the malady his shriveled body holds.

A railway porter in red,

with students around his hospital bed,

the swelling in his groin,

their moment of delight.

A newly married couple,

celebrating joyfully,

the birth,

of their lovely baby girl.

A boy of five,

with swelling over his eyes,

looking sick and sullen,

his mother worrisome.

A girl of eight,

with obvious pain,

and an illiterate dad,

sickling crisis yet again.

A man of fifty,

with severe chest pain and sweaty,

with not enough money (for the injection),

the last day of his journey.

The hospital thus a cacophony,

of sick and cured,

doctors and nurses,

in clinics, theatres and wards.

9

Cinquain- Caring, Chaos, Conflict

Poetry can illuminate the artistic side of medicine. It allows one to express oneself and fosters creativity. The views one espouses about phenomenon in medicine can be succinctly expressed through poetry.[1] It lends clarity to the expression of one's experiences and emotions.

Violence against doctors is a global phenomenon [3,4] In India, it has assumed alarming proportions. This poem highlights the myriads of factors at play in precipitating the violence. Public hospitals in India are overcrowded and understaffed. Equipments are faulty and many vital investigations are not available.

Cinquain [cinq (French) = five] is a form of poetry that uses a five-line stanza. Each line is made up of a certain number of syllables in the following order: two, four, six, eight, and two. The first line introduces the subject, which is then described in the next three lines of the stanza, and the cinquain ends with a reference to the subject again. I chose this poetic expression for its simplicity and its ability to crisply [2] convey the message. To add fuel to the angst against doctors, is a faulty belief system. It is believed that malpractice is rampant, and that doctors in public hospitals are deliberately derelict in their duties. The recent physical violence against an intern in Kolkata is testimony to this trend. Large scale protests by doctors, including a nation-wide strike, has brought the issue into the limelight. Such patient behavior is highly condemnable and needs to be curbed immediately.[5]

Bromberg R. Poetry and Medicine. Medscape J Med. 2008;10(3):63.

Dhaliwal U. Syllabic medicine (Cinquain). CHRISMED J Health Res.2018; 5:305-6.

Wyatt R, Anderson-Drevs K, Van Male LM. Workplace violence in health care: a critical issue with a promising solution. JAMA. 2016;316(10):1037-8.

Kasai Y, Mizuno T, Sakakibara T, Thu S, Kyaw TA, Htun KA. A survey of workplace violence against physicians in the hospitals, Myanmar. BMC Res Notes. 2018;11(1):133. doi: 10.1186/ s13104-018-3240-x.

Ghosh K. Violence against doctors- a wake- up call. Indian J Med Res. 2018;148(2):130-3

Patients

Rustic, Naive

Pleading, Wailing, Fuming

Desperate for cure

Helpless…

Clinics

Overcrowded Doctors,

nurses scurry

Wretched place for the sick

Chaos

Doctors

Resource hit

Persevering, Struggling

Lifesavers against odds

Copers…

Talking

Short, Curt

Incoherent, inept

Telling briefly confusingly

Lacking…

Conflict

False Notions

Impatience flaring

Diverging expectations

Wanton…

(Paralikar, S. (2019). Caring, chaos, conflict - a cinquain. Research and Humanities in Medical Education, 6, 61–62. Retrieved from https://www.rhime.in/ojs/index.php/rhime/article/view/227)

1 0

My first patient

We were nineteen years old,

budding to be doctors.

We ambled into the outpatient department,

where the perplexing sequence would unfold.

We were nineteen years old,

and waiting to examine

a real patient in the hospital

on our own.

We were nineteen years old,

And naïve to the societal intricacies.

The poor teaming nation we were then,

had seemingly tragic fallacies.

We were nineteen years old,

and came a poor adolescent girl,

with massive splenomegaly,

which was brutally burnt.

We were nineteen years old,

And hopelessly perplexed,

at the patient

we had just witnessed.

We were nineteen years old,

and troubled by the junior doctor's outburst:

He scolded the guardian in terse words,

making a mockery of the suffering of the girl.

We were nineteen years old,

and naïve to professional conduct,

we were witness to an interaction,

that was truly transformational.

Rather than empathy and compassion,

the doctor emanated disdain and frustration,

his motives though honest,

his manner brazenly incorrect.

Such was the (mis) fortune,

of the teeming millions in our midst,

abdominal pain rather than being treated with pills

a quack could cruelly burn the spot instead!

Years have elapsed since such turn,

quacks unleashing burns,

though still abound in our midst,

now docs are present to provide basic care at least!

11

Dear Student in Distress

You claim that time is scanty,

to scan Gray and Guyton,

but you while it away

fidgeting through your phone,

and indulging in

frivolous talk,

with your mates,

at your place.

You claim that teaching is boring,

and lectures useless,

but you don't care for the one,

for whom it is a passion:

His message clear,

his hour interesting,

his notes meticulous,

the subject now glorious.

All you care is for the pass fare!

You claim that the facilities

are frugal and faulty.

Yet whose fault it is,

when you make sullen environments shoddy:

With your awful habits,

carelessness and callousness thrown in;

remember the boy with the oil lamp,

who has already made your camp.

You claim that opportunities are fleeting,

yet you are now gifted one,

but you bask in the glory of the seat,

rather than study and be erudite;

you want a life as well,

but where's the discipline,

to burn the midnight oil,

right when the semester begins!

Thus, my boys and girls,

it comes in a package:

make the most of the master,

forget the rest, lest they falter;

means may be frugal and faulty,

use them with prudence,

practice perseverance,

it's a fact:

That diamonds emerge from dust.

1 2

My Protege

He sneaks in my office searching eyes,

wondering whether I would be nice.

I welcome him with a friendly smile,

which to him is utter surprise.

I befriend him with some banter,

only to be astounded,

by the odds,

he has encountered.

Next, he speaks with searching eyes,

 wondering whether it would be wise:

to reveal his utter befuddlement,

at the state of the medical college.

He just limits to some queries,

in a chapter,

he read just yesterday,

amidst the disarray.

Next, he speaks with searching eyes,

wondering whether this is the moment precise:

to reveal unashamedly that he just can't cope,

looking for a ray of hope.

He reveals his predicament,

in bits and pieces,

which I duly acknowledge,

as genuine.

Next, we are friends forever though,

times are a changing,

seasons,

come and go.

I teach him the Pomodoro,

and Mind Mapping on the go.

He now looks to be up to date,

until he resigns to his fate.

It is imperative that he falls behind,

then there is falling,

Of a different kind.

His eyes have met the love of his life,

he has fallen in love,

which has resulted in,

some serious strife.

It is then that we burst into

giggles,

and embrace the reality,

to become mates permanent.

This is his acid test,

he aces it with grit,

the lovely lady,

is surely in.

So goes on the tale,

between me and him,

now, sometimes we meet,

only in the canteen.

I have done my job with honesty,

without hope of any bounty.

Then I get my ultimate reward,

when he proclaims to all:

This is the one,

who made me a man,

otherwise, I would only be an also ran!

13

A Push to Freedom

I stumbled upon

a boy of twenty,

distraught with thoughts

seething anxiety.

I probed him,

on his malady,

He went to unravel,

his burning OCD.

He was treated well,

by some good doc;

 While he paddled on,

he came upon a rock.

There was the

omnipresent disease,

obsessions and compulsions

the emperor of all neurosis.

I lent him a hand,

lest he could fly again;

 He responded gallantly,

my altruism not in vain.

There was this psychiatrist,

whose therapy was goldilocks.

I am yet to see,

such a prudent doc.

Finally, he is free of

all ills and pills;

It was a triumph,

of wisdom and will.

14

Student X

Because from the hinterlands he had sauntered,

because he had a lecture theatre to endure,

because of his evening meal he was not sure,

because he had to fall in line with peers,

because he had to endure the filth of the hostel,

because 'work hard' was his only gospel,

because as a doctor he would be lacking in skills,

because he would be at a loss for professional traits:

We should solemnly christen him student X!

15

Suicide

Stress, stress and hopes betrayed,

he finally fails in the final test,

making him dreary and dour,

he now must face his family's scourge.

There is a minute matter,

his brain gone bonkers,

he thus thinks tonight

logic and rationale remain behind.

There he thinks twice

about his faulty fate:

None to care and cast a concern,

it's a nadir he now can't just navigate.

That is when he steps up,

this is his final bluff,

the setting sun scripts a sorry tale,

for him it will never rise again

16

Beating Procrastination

I put off studying,

biochemistry for the next day.

As days turn to weeks,

I freeze in fear and dismay.

Thus, goes the saga:

Between me and biochemistry,

when will I begin,

is yet a mystery.

Now the biochemistry exam is next week,

as sweat trickles down my forehead,

and my heart skips a beat:

I begin to yearn,

hope I started studying biochemistry,

when the semester began.

Luckily, I have come across,

literature on procrastination:

I know now,

that this habit can be beaten.

It is necessary,

to exercise willpower:

When the cue,

beckons in the form of a trigger:

That could be a racing heart,

which might dissuade me,

from taking up,

biochemistry.

Then there's the core belief:

That I'm not good enough at biochemistry;

Those memories are as fresh as the greens,

when I squeezed in sleep between chemistry pages.

I need to be firm,

ensure that my mood,

if not sunny,

is not gloomy.

Finally, it's necessary to

focus on the process,

rather than the product.

Biochemistry must be learnt (bit by bit),

Comprising a journey:

Let it be later,

Rather than always falter.

II
MIND

17

Can I carry on?

I had arrived with supreme confidence and pomp,

the sophomore,

now a physician,

wears a look forlorn.

My mind wanders,

as the patients sauntered,

I care for them,

braving the ruthless system.

I am reluctantly drawn,

to blame myself,

for the travesty that prevails.

Patients in hoards,

day in and out,

drugs and disposables,

at times, out of sight.

The Foley's is not there or has a hole,

the superior seldom heed,

my troubled discourse.

I try to draw,

all my energies:

But they do not answer my call,

yet I must carry on.

The patient is a case,

on paper and in person:

I push

Myself along,

I wonder:

How long,

can I carry on?

Joshi A, Paralikar S, Kataria S, Kalra J, Harkunni S, Singh T. Poetry in medicine: A pedagogical tool to foster empathy among medical students and health care professionals. Journal of Poetry Therapy. 2022 Apr 3;35(2):85-97

18

To Obsessive Compulsive Disorder

You were my bete noire...

The swirling thoughts in my jelly;

I tried to wish you away...

You swirled more ferociously,

 heralding tragedy.

You were capricious...

In one guise

or the other,

I knew you were part of me,

yet I despised you,

heralding anarchy.

You made me lose my mind...

I became a different being.

I could no longer ace the test:

Doomed to fail;

Far behind the rest.

You made me lose sight

of the environ

all of a sudden:

I struggled to be social,

A misfit in the middle:

My circumstances became perilous.

You were my bête noire...

I yearned

for a win over you:

I banged on every door

I could,

yet you would not lose.

You beat the shrink too...

even he couldn't decipher it;

Who were you?

Wrong cures and advice

led me to a precipice.

You were my bête noire...

However, the cure

lay in a distant land.

I trudged warily,

a flickering ray of hope,

then shone brightly.

You have been reined in...

An eclectic mix of pills and will

Perfectly proportioned

 seems to be your foil.

It's been a lost decade,

you played well,

but my perseverance prevailed.

(Paralikar, S. (2021). To Obsessive Compulsive Disorder. *Research and Humanities in Medical Education*, 8, 69–70. Retrieved from https://www.rhime.in/ojs/index.php/rhime/article/view/486)

19

During my blues

I had the blues

when I was twenty;

a hurricane struck,

and bizarre thoughts ran amuck.

Yet my buddies turned a blind eye;

I wish I'd had them by my side.

I had the blues

and the shrinks were naïve:

they prescribed before giving a full ear.

Then, the thoughts got stronger.

And still my buddies turned a blind eye;

I wish they'd stuck by my side.

I had the blues

when exams hovered,

and the thoughts wouldn't be dispelled,

focusing on intricate concepts was too much to expect.

Yet, even then, my buddies turned a blind eye.

I wish I'd had them by my side.

I had the blues

because my professors didn't uncover

the soul of my predicament,

and blamed me for my plight instead.

Yet, again, my buddies turned a blind eye.

I wish I'd had them by my side.

I had the blues

as I waged a lonely battle.

And when I emerged a bruised victor,

I wondered whether I deserved to suffer.

 While my buddies, they turned a blind eye;

I wish I'd had them by my side.

I still have the blues

because my mind meanders over what could have been,

had circumstances been favorable.

And as I wage my lonely battle,

even today my buddies turn a blind eye,

when all I need is to be seen as:

 worthy and not cast aside.

(Paralikar, S. (2023). During my blues. *Research and Humanities in Medical Education*, *10*, 15–16. Retrieved from https://www.rhime. in/ojs/index.php/rhime/article/view/563)

20

Misery and Remedy

I would wake up past the midnight hour,

and wonder about the next day so sour,

 that I then drudged drearily along,

rather than, up and about like a song.

This routine

got all too long.

My genuine history,

consigned as a weary monologue.

Days were gone, and years passed,

my eyes weary and silken hair lost,

all opportunity seemed an impossible probability,

my lonely life itself now a calamity.

My soul and soma,

 both needed a repair,

I yearned for a magic pill,

that would save the day.

The sun did shine beyond the horizon,
 somebody did prescribe pills with precision.
 Then I slept dreaming gladly,
waking up again in glee, rather than agony.
 As weeks turned to months and then a
 year, my ravaged brain had surely been
repaired, by pills designed especially,
for those who had my malady.

As I look up and above,
I wonder why I suffered till now.
There was always this pill in the neighborhood store,
 for prescribing it passed opportunities galore.
Somebody may call this sheer 'luck',
maybe I missed a trick as much,
but the tale should never be the same,
for all those sick and in grievous pain.

2 1

To My Asperger's

You are my true self,

that sets me apart from the rest:

Though blessed with boundless intellect,

amiss is the human connect.

You are my true self,

the charioteer of my Rosie Projects.

I am the little erudite professor,

as predicted by the angelic Asperger.

You are my true self,

that falters at everyday emotions;

though empathy is so innate,

I struggle to demonstrate it yet.

You are my true self,

that makes my social being falter:

Often it is a void,

and sometimes in the abyss.

You are my true self,

that driver of my creative endeavors,

which make me a shining star,

in the galaxy of pious people.

You are my true self,

as I navigate the choppy waters;

You make me so diverse,

I truly ponder whether you are a divine boon or destiny's curse?

22

To Post-Traumatic Stress Disorder

The black years of the black era,

that glitter like yesterday,

worsening evening and Sundays,

unlike a champion's memorabilia.

The days flash fearfully,

during vivid dreams daily,

my nights hardly free,

to sleep peacefully.

It is not that I do not toil,

through the sunny afternoons,

it's that when I rest,

that the memories flash.

Now that I am forty-eight,

weary I sometimes get,

easily,

a window for them to slide in effortlessly.

Thus, goes the dance,

between me and my dark days,

I am seemingly amid,

that tragedy always.

23

Amiss – A Cinquain

Patient,

Is Anxious,

Needs an urgent remedy,

Cure often amiss,

Tragic.

Doctor,

Dys-competent;

Fault seeking, just giving a pill,

Talk therapy just a talk,

Wanton.

Society,

just ignorant.

Wrong beliefs, faulty labels,

Stigma, pervasive,

Disdain.

Drugs,

seldom cures.

Side effects bothersome;

Docs' only arsenal,

Not yet.

Life,

Broken.

Patient troubled, yet trudges on;

Often close to a cure.

Steep.

24

The Fallout of Ruffled Feathers

The day before has been a bit sour,
 relationships ruffled suddenly.
I worry about my work, then every hour,
going to bed in a cacophony of confusion.

The sun rises and sleep has been fleeting,
it's then the poise takes a deadly beating,
Anxiety builds up, escalating into panic,
now I am obsessed about the future - ruminating.

The bed seems cosier, I am drowsy,
yet my laden legs, make it to the toilet.
Then I make frivolous complaints, to myself and others,
 about the grievous past, that heralded this ill fate.

It's phones ringing, asking for unavailable help,

none willing to listen to me wail.

It's then that I reach the absolutely nadir,

as the world is surely crumbling.

It's been an arduous toil,

To avail such a misfortune.

Hope flickers like a distant star,

there are strategies to make it through…

25

STIGMA

For several years

around me,

clouds darkened:

Making life miserable and

real progress difficult.

Amid the storm,

I would seek your assistance,

to calm the weather.

Some of you were erudite

and graceful,

treating me with respect

and equity.

But the wanton folks outnumbered you,

making a mockery of my blues.

There were times when

I was just cast aside,

my wanton abilities,

viewed suspiciously

by the wanton tribe.

The nudges and nays

were subtle and silent,

yet they pierced my ears.

I wondered when the dark clouds

would turn orange

my blues vanishing away,

so that your banishing

could cease someday.

The scar thus formed

flares every evening,

making me look for soothing

and friendship.

It's been an arduous endeavor,

to put myself together,

lest your banishment

altogether disappear.

26

Bye-Bye OCD-I (Cinquain)

Doctor

erudite

trained well, able

good communicator, affable

expert.

New pill

prescribed

brain changes felt

just right augmentation

Magic.

Symptoms

just minimal

now fleeting, transient

emotional stability

trace.

Stigma

subsides bit

new friends welcoming

stable relationships, banter crescent.

Function

more productive

less stress, cope well

more flow possible nowadays

better.

27

Bye-Bye OCD-II (Haiku)

No opportunity,
amidst my OCD,
magic pill given.

Tough year passes by
entire brain restructured,
healthy once again.

World seen afresh,
new social experiments,
umpteen mistakes.

Covert compulsions,
stop occurring,
with apt strategy.

Rejuvenation,
of soul and soma is done,
ill gone, new sojourn.

III

Pandemic

28

Awakening-I (Cinquain)

Virus

Disease, Death

Fear, Panic, Despair, Hope

Global pandemic

Wily.

Life

Ordinary, Fragile

Virus forces the realization

Doubtful future

Chaos.

Lockdown

Chats are now live

Eyes meet, Emotions vent

Blessing in disguise

Chance.

Money

Useless Paper

Fruits of endeavor, toil

 Brings little comfort

Barter

Matters

Big vs Small

Family, Friends, Peers, Neighbors

Bonding, cherishing

Woken

29

Awakening-II

Beware Corona!

You might be the latest one,

but for eons

sapiens have been plagued

by other 'black deaths'

- Cholera and Malaria –

And we found a way (out)

through Leeuwenhoek's eager perseverance,

through Snow's flawless organization,

Through Fleming's chance observation.

Now it's your turn, devious Corona!

You try to be Man's bete noire;

But we, with intellect and compassion,

will find our way,

through means tried and tested,

new therapies and pills

which soon will be

invented.

- Beware Corona —

You're the latest one

and may not be the last

But you shall be overcome,

for we're in this - all of us together - to win!

Paralikar, S. (2020). Awakening. *Research and Humanities in Medical Education*, 7, 60–61. Retrieved from https://www.rhime.in/ojs/index.php/rhime/article/view/287

3 0

Two men who met a different fate

Blip! Blip! Blip,

Peeks the notification.

I soon make a video call

and ask a few questions,

help me zero in,

On the seventy-five-year old's condition.

His anxious son,

tells me about this tendency

to sniff.

Oh! I am alarmed,

at the urgency

now of the situation.

Fever, cough and low saturation,

with supplementary oxygen,

coupled with chronic bronchitis,

Make me realize,

That he needs to be wheeled

to the nearest facility.

The hapless son,

also caring for an ailing mother,

and concerned about the lack of cash,

compelled to care at home,

the troubled family loses the elderly one.

Blip! Blip! Blip!

Peeks the notification.

I soon make a video call,

and zero in,

on the seventy-five-year old's condition.

His middle- aged son,

tells me about his bronchitis,

fever, cough and supplementary oxygen,

make a perilous concoction;

With oxygen saturation edgy,

 he needs to be wheeled in,

to a nearby hospital.

The son hangs up,

and decides on a private consultation,

his bronchitis and COVID both reined in

a couple of days in,

The cash was there,

and that's the difference:

One received the needed attention,

the other helplessly surrendered!

Loneliness

In the brimming spring of January,

the wily virus struck stealthily,

 bringing to its knees,

cities big and small,

loneliness, a by-product,

of a system now defunct.

There were no friends for banter,

no parties for dinner,

no malls to saunter.

The wily virus had cast a spell,

being lonely with my family,

I kept busy with tasks mundane.

While I waited for my turn,

and eerily hoped that

I would always overcome,

I egged on with resilience,

a ray of hope always

lay behind the horizon.

As the months elapsed,

the virus did decay,

I was alive and well,

my resilience,

had beaten the virus,

and its wily spell.

Though you may be lonely,

keep busy,

and seek small victory.

Remember! Such adversity will be overcome,

you must demonstrate character and resilience,

that is the prescription for each and everyone.

3 2

My Corona diary

I am forty-five,

and my life is in full bloom;

Devious Corona has struck,

it's day two with fever.

I wonder whether I will get back ever,

to the life I worked so hard for over the years.

I am forty-five,

and today is day five.

My body is warm as water is

in the morning.

My doctors tell me:

It's a bit of a warning.

I am forty-five,

and today is day seven,

on steroids,

the cough persists:

I wonder whether the Koch's I had before,

would make things run amiss.

I am forty-five,

And day ten is when my sacs,

are filled with fluid:

it's an emergency rush to the hospital,

 where's the oxygen bottle?

That will help me battle (devious Corona).

I am forty-five,

and running from here to there,

in search of ephemeral air:

Finally, there's oxygen,

I can breathe well,

while the dutiful doctors,

nurse me cautiously back to health.

White Curtain

I remember so vividly,

you smiled away,

as I gently unraveled

 concepts of physiology.

Your smile,

your approval,

contentment,

the prize of my toil.

Now you are draped

in those gears,

they call 'masks'

masking your precious smile,

and approval,

and contentment.

I wonder how long

it will last,

this mask of yours

and you're hiding from me.

denying me,

the prize of my toil.

IV
METAPHORS

3 4

Ode to the Heart

I love the way

you lie ensconced,

comfortable, though within a cage;

your actions are selfless,

devotion single-minded.

I love your design,

so simple,

yet so precise;

galloping incessantly,

you are always on time.

I love your poetry,

the signal from your battery

that courses through cables;

a beautiful machine,

elegant, and able.

I love your mystic melody,

played by channels like 'funny';

keeping pitch and tune,

you orchestrate the ions,

 out and in.

I love your eternal lust,

for precious calcium;

playing hide and seek,

leaving enough in abeyance,

for another occasion.

I love your synchronous rhythm,

like the cadence of horses galloping.

the opening and closing

of the valves

with an equestrian's precision.

I love the powerful pump you are,

using your chambers

to generate a life force;

urging the blood to traverse

the entire course.

I love the way you regulate

the vascular pressure:

you make redundant saviors,

showcasing the Comroe principle

in full splendor.

I love your courtesy,

how you politely enable

baroreceptors and renin

to rein you in.

I love the way,

you relentlessly toil;

like a child of the soil,

who battles perennial

floods and famine.

I love your instinct for survival

against your own follies,

and against sapiens' eternal enemies

- fat and sugar -

the harbingers of all misery.

I love your faithfulness,

to me and to others;

you are vulnerable,

yet so reliable;

a true mate always!

(Paralikar, S. (2021). Ode to the heart. *Research and Humanities in Medical Education*, 8, 125–126. Retrieved from https://www.rhime.in/ojs/index.php/rhime/article/view/521)

3 5

A Runner's Heart

POET'S NOTE:

MBBS students are taught about the cardiovascular response to exercise during their classes on the cardiovascular system in Physiology. The topic helps to give them a bird's eye view of the integrative aspects of cardiovascular functions. The following poem is an attempt to aid understanding and recall by replacing a typical cognitive exercise with a catchy verse using a hypothetical athlete as an anchor.

'I want to run,' says the athlete.

'Wait a bit,' retorts his heart.

'I need to get ready for it.'

The sympathetic discharges,

and the athlete's heart races:

a stronger pump it has become.

It makes red elixir run

through arteries and veins,

which dilate as metabolites accumulate.

The blood rapidly darts

back to the heart:

aided by three efficient pumps.

Skeletal, abdominal and thoracic:

while the first pump propels it,

the latter two pull it all in.

The toiling heart

demands more fuel,

so that it can fulfill its part.

The coronaries oblige,

as the elixir arrives,

with oxygen that the twin sacs provide.

This synchronized symphony,

this practiced drill,

is as necessary as it is beautiful.

If not for the cooperation

of the heart, lungs and vessels,

the athlete would be left far behind.

The following is a summary of the cardiovascular changes during exercise:

At the beginning of exercise, increased sympathetic activity causes tachycardia.

Increased ventricular contractility causes the heart to pump more blood.

The cardiac output - the blood pumped out by the heart per minute - increases from 5L/min to 20-25L/min.

Due to release of vasodilator metabolites like adenosine, lactic acid, and CO_2, the blood vessels in the skeletal muscles dilate.

The venous return increases aided by the skeletal muscle, and abdominal and thoracic pumps.

(Paralikar, S. (2017). A runner's heart. *Research and Humanities in Medical Education*, 4, 42–43. Retrieved from https://www.rhime. in/ojs/index.php/rhime/article/view/112)

36

Ode to the Brain

You are the peerless conductor,

of the symphony:

The human being,

in all his unique splendor.

Your surface resembles a plateau,

with hillocks and valleys,

yet within the deep recesses,

hide uncanny mysteries.

You are the one,

that enables consciousness:

which enables speech and memory,

intellect and empathy.

You are the one,

that makes us truly human.

Without your deftness,

we would lose ourselves!

37

Cursed Commodity

The dowry days,
were for all to see:
Burnt women
in the emergency.

Body became corpse like,
women wailed in pain,
we watched helplessly,
such a sight again and again.

Some preliminary treatment,
and transfer to the burns ward,
 with the husband absconding,
what would become of her ward?

That was the state of the society then,
women were commodities,
marriage was the means,
for it to be exchanged.

3 8

The Il- Fated Patient

The uneven clouds shut out the sun,

the room was damp and squib,

there lay a man still,

wondering what of him had become?

I hesitantly prodded him for his history,

he narrated his grievous tale:

He had visited hospitals galore,

wondering why he had been stuck with such tragedy?

Then he came upon this good doctor,

who discovered a malignant liver.

his eyes signaled betrayal,

as he wondered why none cared before.

I departed with a sour taste,

keeping in mind his disdain:

For docs who prescribed erroneous pills,

didn't he deserve a better fate?

3 9

Ulcers

I scampered every dawn
 to be with the junior doc,
 rows of wounded folks,
littered the stinging wards.

There were varied ulcers,
 displaying a fashion parade,
only they signaled squalor and disease,
beneath the dirty mattresses' creases.

The doc tended them roughly,
 agony lent a tear often.
The antiseptic drooling,
bandages needed slight tightening.

The doc had to complete
his job at eight.
he scampered through the ulcers,
looking for 'good' patients.

Men with pennies,

would withstand these halls,

they had an offer not to be refused:

Either the limb would be amputed

or healed to be reused.

40

Physiology

Because it describes the milieu,

 which makes me and you;

Because it unravels the processes,

That ensure homeostasis.

Because it is a window to the cells,

that are the units of life itself,

Because Guyton and Vander,

have narrated it in its full splendor;

Because it describes precisely,

How man survives.

Because it is the logic of life,

The basis for normal and abnormal alike;

Because bereft of it,

medicine would be just another baseless fit.

Because it is how we understand life:

That physiology is my chosen tribe!

4 1

The Organ Supreme

Because it is so intricate,

because it has the function to regulate:

The most vital of all parameters:

 Blood pressure,

Because it maintains the balance,

between acid and base.

Because it enables,

survival even in the desert.

Because it rains in potassium,

the diabolical one.

Because it rids the body

of all the waste generates;

Because it synthesizes the one,

that leads to the creation of

red blood corpuscles.

Because it harnesses sunlight,

so that calcium confers us might;

Because it is so vital,

That bereft of it,

the heart would fail,

and brain would swell,

or shrink:

So imminent would-be death,

that it is the organ supreme:

The one that maintains the milieu:

that Canon christened 'homeostasis.'

42

Genes: Miscreants meet their Match

Your mom and dad love you so much,

but they may also screw you up,

passing along the bad, with the good,

while lacing the former with surer stuff.

Ensconced on beads arranged in a double helix,

right ones create melody,

wrong ones the fallacies,

that are the epitome of disease.

There is the fable of Watson and Crick,

who sauntered along with Maurice Wilkins,

to decipher the code of life,

on which the genes reside.

Man is a mere spectator,

as they cast their spell:

A legend is the sickle cell,

But Huntington is the cruelest of the clan!

Now is the era of gene editing,

as Doudna has deciphered a patch:

That repairs miscreant genes,

ushering a new dawn to rid us of genetic ills!

43

Why do the Humanities Matter?

I am a relentlessly innovative one:

I began with the knowledge

that the planets

Go round the sun.

Now I have come up

With incredibly smart tablets for fun,

and lovely cars that run,

without reckless drivers.

Hence, arises the question:

In this maddening era of machines,

where do I sync:

The human?

Science, technology, engineering and math are the future:

Robots are running riot,

but where's the empathy,

but where's the connect,

that each tiny interaction requires?

There lies the need for a human face,

as to him empathy is innate.

The doctor needs to have the right mental frame

and demonstrate compassion as well.

This he can do effortlessly,

with his empathetic self.

For these vital attributes:

Arts, poetry,

literature, history,

drama, melody:

Has been incorporated into the

medicos' study.

Thus, the medical curriculum,

becomes even more,

Fun to learn.

44

A Late Betrayal

I am in my fifth decade,

yet I have already

begun to fade.

As I have a herd to care,

I wonder:

how can I now afford to falter?

I am in my fifth decade,

And I am plagued with

weird ways:

My fingers saunter,

suddenly at rest:

The epitome of my crooked fate.

I am in my fifth decade,

and I falter,

during tender talks,

with my near ones:

all alarmed,

at my stutter and the commotion.

I am in my fifth decade,

my gene's betrayal,

Has left me dry:

My memory falters,

at every turn:

My persona now shaken.

I am in my fifth decade,

my kids wonder:

whether they will be next?

My gene's betrayal,

is a dominant one,

my kids' fate may be just as cruel.

I am in my fifth decade,

my gene's betrayal,

is a wicked twist:

with a family and their kids,

I only wish,

it had manifested in my twenties.

POET'S NOTE:

Huntington's disease is a rare, genetic disease (affecting 5 out of 1,00,000 people worldwide), which usually manifests in the fifth decade of life. By this time, the patient has already started a family. This is precisely one of the reasons as to why it has earned the disrepute of being called 'the cruellest' disease known to man [1,2].

Huntington's disease is caused by degeneration of neurons in the striatum, which is a part of the basal ganglia of the brain. There are also degenerative changes in the frontal and temporal cortices of the brain. The abnormal gene responsible for this disease is located on chromosome 4. The gene codes for Huntingtin, a protein of unknown function. The spectrum of symptoms in Huntington's disease are broad. It includes chorea (rapid involuntary dancing) movements, cognitive symptoms and psychiatric disturbances. Speech becomes slurred and progressive dementia is followed by death [3,4].

REFERENCES:

Krebs C, Weinberg J, Akeeson E. The Basal Ganglia In: Krebs C, Weinberg J, Akeeson E, editors. Lippincott's Illustrated Reviews Neuroscience. Baltimore: Lippincott Williams and Wilkins; 2012, pp 321.

Genova L. Inside the O' Briens. Gallery Books: New York (Kindle edition)

Barrett E, Barman S, Brooks H, Yuan J. Reflex and Voluntary Control of Posture and Movement. In: Barrett E, Barman S, Brooks H, Yuan J. eds. Ganong's Review of Medical Physiology.

New York: Ganong's Review of Medical Physiology, 26th edition, 2019. pp 241.

www.mayoclinic.org/diseases-conditions/huntingtons- disease/symptoms-causes/syc-20356117 (Last accessed on 27th May 2021).

45

Misery Unleashed by the Messenger

I am sixty-five,

and I had been betrayed

by the inkblots

that lie deep

within the recesses

of the three- pound mass

within my vault.

Dopamine:

the messenger for pleasure,

and locomotion,

was the chief culprit:

having decided to work less:

maybe go on a strike,

causing all the strife.

I am sixty-five,

and when I would be still,

my fingers would keep on moving,

like a sewing machine.

My face sunken and stiff,

they call 'mask' like,

hardly evoked emotions.

I am sixty-five,

and my arms were stiff,

like wood

in winter.

And my walk was straight

as a rod,

as my arms refused to sway like yours.

I am sixty-five,

And they prescribed,

Dopamine,

To relieve my misery.

Finally, electricity deep within the recess

has eased the condition.

I am fine now.

But I wonder about the millions,

still waiting

to be towed!

POET'S NOTE:

James Parkinson, in 1817, described a 'shaking palsy' in humans. The disease affects mostly men above 65 years of age. It is characterized by resting (pill-rolling) tremor, akinesia and rigidity in the limbs. The constellation of symptoms occurs due to the premature degeneration of dopaminergic neurons in the substantia nigra (in the basal ganglia) of the brain.

46

The College

Into the heavenly abode,

a place so cold,

bodies:

With a stench of formalin,

squalor and dirt supreme.

I bore it all,

with tears and mirth,

for it gave birth,

to me, a doc.

47

The Resident

Upright,

tight-lipped,

lecturing straight from the book:

Still needs to have a look,

at patients,

with patience:

rather than rush through the hour,

and a condescending manner.

He has his girl,

she has her boy,

and the two hearts flirt,

with slender mirth.

Burnout and bored,

three months more,

the exams are a drill,

life begins.

48

The Canteen

A place teeming,

with students,

munching,

drinking,

searching,

dating.

The tables being half half-sanitized,

some ostracized.

A place not a fit,

for the students' canteen.

Teachers

Teachers aloof,

ignorant to many cues.

Erudite few,

teach with passion,

but where is the scholarly approach?

Students learn by self,

why so many to teach, then?

The Exams

Tension and stress,

a rat race:

For post-graduation entry,

robbing it of its vitality.

The formative ones,

ought to help them learn,

but they exaggerate the burn,

until he burns out,

and is laid in the ward.

The construct is

fuzzy,

validity is the tragedy.

It is feasible,

Yet does it have objectivity?

Making a mockery,

of utility.

Baroreceptors

The blood pumped out by the heart,

Returns via the veins:

It thus goes round,

again and again.

It gently tucks the baroreceptors

in the peeping carotid sinus

and the mighty arch of aorta:

they sense the blood pressure,

and relay it to the medulla.

When you rise,

from a chair:

The blood pools lazily

in the leg veins.

this lowers the vital pressure,

causing the receptors to fire,

vigorously to the brain,

Up goes the sympathetic,

the heart races a bit.

The ventricles now a stronger pump

as the blood

gushes right up to the cerebrum.

When the pressure stays up,

long enough:

The receptors give up:

They reset.

Leaving it for the kidney

to set it straight.

Thus, pressure is held,

second by second:

critically relying,

on the baroreceptors' signal.

5 2

Fix the lecture

Lectures of today,

Useless and boring:

The sage on the stage:

Is relentlessly narrating.

Yet they help in coverage of the topic,

oh! the sage acquires precious expertise.

lectures may help in understanding complex concepts,

that students are also motivated is an advantage.

Passivity and compliance,

no critical thinking and problem solving;

Because adults learn better by doing,

such lectures are not interesting.

Lectures need to be interactive

learning needs to be active:

Make students work with the content of the lecture,

this is the template

for the future.

Buzz groups and brainstorming,

one minute paper and asking questions.

As students are doing,

learning is better and interesting.

Lectures are here to stay,

do not cast them aside.

Rather than the sage on the stage,

be the guide on the side.

POET'S NOTE:

Lectures are taken in all medical and allied sciences. Their utility lies in them enabling coverage of the topic and understanding of concepts. In addition, students are motivated to study.

The traditional method of delivering lectures is called 'the sage on the stageapproach.' The lecturer transmits information and the students are just passive recipients. In fact, a famous quote states that, "Lecture is a method by which the notes of the teacher are passed to the student without passing through the minds of either." As a result, students hardly develop the skill of 'thinking on the go' which is vital for a physician. No wonder, lectures are considered as boring and useless.

The key to fix the lecture is to use active learning strategies such as questioning, brainstorming, buzz groups, one minute paper. Thus, teaching in consonance with the principles of adult learning will enable the students to learn in a fun and interesting manner. As there is a dearth of faculty across the country, it would be prudent to state that lectures are here to stay. Hence, the above-mentioned strategies, which help in making lectures effective, are the need of the hour.

5 3

Rules for Power Point

There are some rules,

you should know,

when you need to

design a power point slideshow.

Simple language

sentences short.

Diagrams to clarify the message,

and preferably only sans serif fonts.

Red is hot,

green and blue are cool,

white is cheerful,

use them depending on the story being told.

Light background with black,

dark one with yellow or blue.

it is most appropriate,

When the number of colors is only one or two.

Sparingly used animations,

diagrams plenty:

To lend clarity,

to any presentation.

This is how it should go,

when you put on the power point slideshow;

Remember! as a teacher you are the key,

the power point is only an accessory

54

Ode to CMCL FAIMER

I love the way,

it emerges from the rusty bowl,

its majesty hidden,

within its walls.

I love the way,

it nurtures,

restless folks like me,

visiting it, itself an epiphany.

I love the way,

the script unfolds,

 the dance with us,

an endless one.

I love the way,

the bar is high.

Reaching it,

is enough of a high.

I love the way,

diverse minds mingle,

Emerging from this

is the 'change' jingle.

I love the way,

Each one of us is molded:

Clay made into finished pots,

which is the ultimate jackpot.

I love the way,

the nuts and bolts,

are tightened and greased,

thus, the gospel disperses.

I love the way,

the orchestra is synced,

I don't proudly proclaim to be a CMCL FAIMERian,

just for the sake of it!

Ode to Baroda

I love your small,

yet boundless spread:

The long roads and deep alleys,

the latter, I never witnessed.

I love your garden

where Adam and Eve meet,

where folks walk merrily,

while the famous sing.

I love your place of learning,

it's art, science and medicine.

The dome that others envy,

and young people's boundless chivalry.

I love your palace:

The epitome of power,

where the captains of music,

famously plied their trade.

I love your folks

erudite most.

courteous and mild,

welcoming all kinds.

I love you most

for to you I belong:

The roads I sauntered,

the scholar rose to doctor.

56

Health

If you get to sixty and beyond,

and can still walk a mile,

without running short of air,

and navigate the day,

albeit with just maladies of today.

You are fit as a stallion,

you must be free of much concern.

If you get to sixty and beyond,

and endure any stress,

without landing in a mess,

and hardly drop a sweat,

and think clearly as well,

and remember memories remote and recent.

Your mind is fit and healthy,

intact is your psychological faculty.

If you are sixty and beyond,

and care about God,

and are not atheist at all,

and are honest and prudent,

you are deemed to be spiritual.

If, by some turn of fate,

you stutter on the road,

yet make a comeback aboard,

you are better than the rest,

you are healthy, my mate.